CLARINET

Broadway's Best

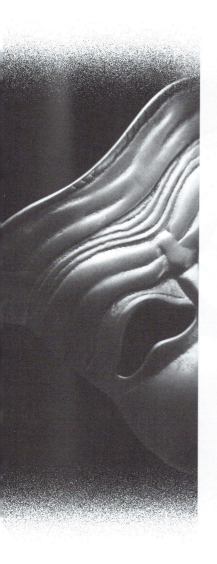

HOW TO USE THE CD ACCOMPANIMENT:
A MELODY CUE APPEARS ON THE RIGHT CHANNEL ONLY. IF YOUR CD PLAYER HAS A BALANCE ADJUSTMENT, YOU CAN ADJUST THE VOLUME OF THE MELODY BY TURNING DOWN THE RIGHT CHANNEL.

ISBN 0-634-08598-0

7777 W. BLUEMOUND RD. P.O. BOX 13819 MILWAUKEE, WI 53213

Visit Hal Leonard Online at
www.halleonard.com

♦ ALWAYS LOOK ON THE BRIGHT SIDE OF LIFE

from SPAMALOT™

Clarinet

Words and Music by
ERIC IDLE

Whistle or play

Whistle or play

ANY DREAM WILL DO

from JOSEPH AND THE AMAZING TECHNICOLOR® DREAMCOAT

Clarinet

Music by ANDREW LLOYD WEBBER
Lyrics by TIM RICE

❸ BRING HIM HOME

from LES MISÉRABLES

Clarinet

Music by CLAUDE-MICHEL SCHÖNBERG
Lyrics by ALAIN BOUBLIL and HERBERT KRETZMER

◆ CAN'T HELP LOVIN' DAT MAN

from SHOW BOAT

Lyrics by OSCAR HAMMERSTEIN II
Music by JEROME KERN

Clarinet

⑤ CASTLE ON A CLOUD

from LES MISÉRABLES

Clarinet

Music by CLAUDE-MICHEL SCHÖNBERG
Lyrics by ALAIN BOUBLIL,
JEAN-MARC NATEL and HERBERT KRETZMER

◆ DANCING QUEEN

from MAMMA MIA

Words and Music by BENNY ANDERSSON,
BJORN ULVAEUS and STIG ANDERSON

Clarinet

Strong Rock

❽ I WHISTLE A HAPPY TUNE

from THE KING AND I

Clarinet

Lyrics by OSCAR HAMMERSTEIN II
Music by RICHARD RODGERS

◆7 GOOD MORNING BALTIMORE

from HAIRSPRAY

Music by MARC SHAIMAN
Lyrics by MARC SHAIMAN and SCOTT WITTMAN

CLARINET

◆⑨ MAMMA MIA

from MAMMA MIA

Words and Music by BENNY ANDERSSON,
BJORN ULVAEUS and STIG ANDERSON

Clarinet

13

MY FAVORITE THINGS

from THE SOUND OF MUSIC

Clarinet

Lyrics by OSCAR HAMMERSTEIN II
Music by RICHARD RODGERS

OL' MAN RIVER

from SHOW BOAT

Lyrics by OSCAR HAMMERSTEIN II
Music by JEROME KERN

CLARINET

Moderately

Banjo

Slower

PUT ON A HAPPY FACE

from BYE BYE BIRDIE

Lyrics by LEE ADAMS
Music by CHARLES STROUSE

Clarinet

WHERE IS LOVE?

from OLIVER!

Words and Music by
LIONEL BART

Clarinet

⟨13⟩ THAT FACE

from THE PRODUCERS

Music and Lyrics by
MEL BROOKS

CLARINET

Slowly and sweetly

◆15 WRITTEN IN THE STARS

from Walt Disney Theatrical Productions' AIDA

CLARINET

Music by ELTON JOHN
Lyrics by TIM RICE

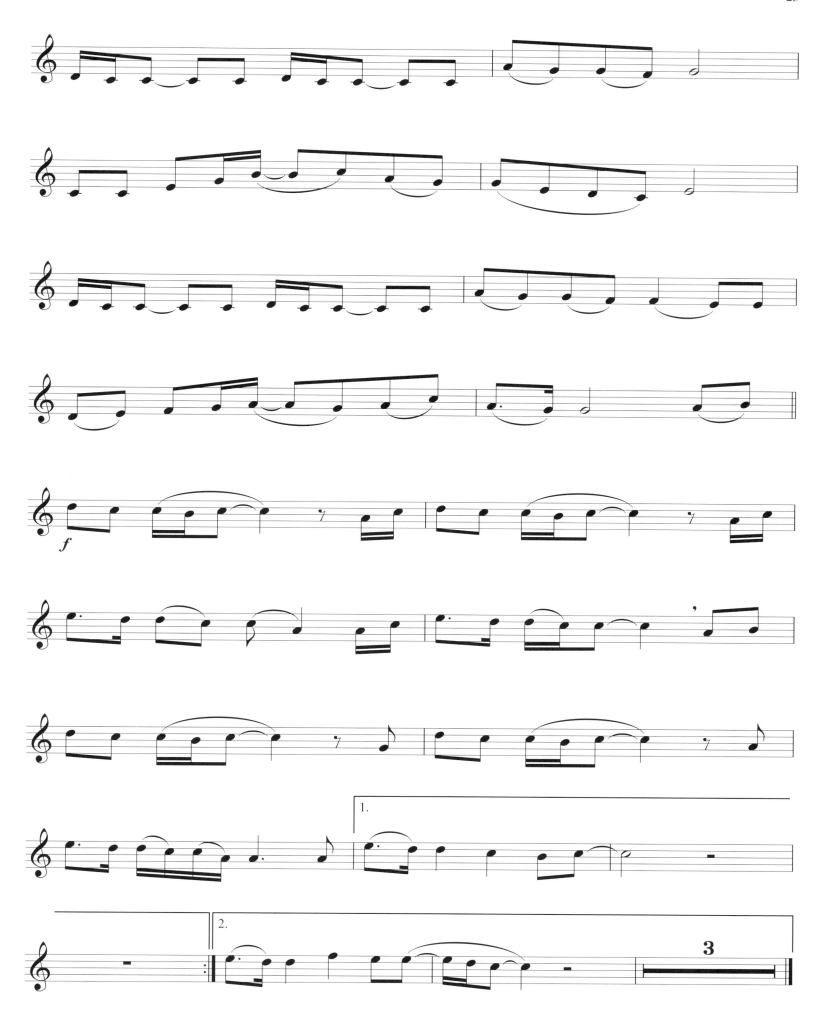

PLAY MORE OF YOUR FAVORITE SONGS

WITH GREAT INSTRUMENTAL PLAY ALONG PACKS FROM HAL LEONARD

Band Jam
12 band favorites complete with accompaniment CD, including: Born to Be Wild • Get Ready for This • I Got You (I Feel Good) • Rock & Roll – Part II (The Hey Song) • Twist and Shout • We Will Rock You • Wild Thing • Y.M.C.A • and more.

00841232	Flute	$10.95
00841233	Clarinet	$10.95
00841234	Alto Sax	$10.95
00841235	Trumpet	$10.95
00841236	Horn	$10.95
00841237	Trombone	$10.95
00841238	Violin	$10.95

Disney Movie Hits
Now solo instrumentalists can play along with a dozen favorite songs from Disney blockbusters, including: Beauty and the Beast • Circle of Life • Cruella De Vil • Go the Distance • God Help the Outcasts • Kiss the Girl • When She Loved Me • A Whole New World • and more.

00841420	Flute	$12.95
00841421	Clarinet	$12.95
00841422	Alto Sax	$12.95
00841423	Trumpet	$12.95
00841424	French Horn	$12.95
00841425	Trombone/Baritone	$12.95
00841686	Tenor Sax	$12.95
00841687	Oboe	$12.95
00841688	Mallet Percussion	$12.95
00841426	Violin	$12.95
00841427	Viola	$12.95
00841428	Cello	$12.95

Disney Solos
An exciting collection of 12 solos with full-band accompaniment on CD. Songs include: Be Our Guest • Can You Feel the Love Tonight • Colors of the Wind • I Just Can't Wait to Be King • Reflection • Under the Sea • You've Got a Friend in Me • Zero to Hero • and more.

00841404	Flute	$12.95
00841405	Clarinet/Tenor Sax	$12.95
00841406	Alto Sax	$12.95
00841407	Horn	$12.95
00841408	Trombone	$12.95
00841409	Trumpet	$12.95
00841410	Violin	$12.95
00841411	Viola	$12.95
00841412	Cello	$12.95
00841506	Oboe	$12.95
00841553	Mallet Percussion	$12.95

FOR MORE INFORMATION, SEE YOUR LOCAL MUSIC DEALER, OR WRITE TO:

HAL•LEONARD CORPORATION
7777 W. BLUEMOUND RD. P.O. BOX 13819 MILWAUKEE, WI 53213

Visit Hal Leonard online at **www.halleonard.com**

Easy Disney Favorites
A fantastic selection of 13 Disney favorites for solo instruments, including: Bibbidi-Bobbidi-Boo • It's a Small World • Let's Go Fly a Kite • Mickey Mouse March • A Spoonful of Sugar • Toyland March • Winnie the Pooh • The Work Song • Zip-A-Dee-Doo-Dah • and many more.

00841371	Flute	$12.95
00841477	Clarinet	$12.95
00841478	Alto Sax	$12.95
00841479	Trumpet	$12.95
00841480	Trombone	$12.95
00841372	Violin	$12.95
00841481	Viola	$12.95
00841482	Cello/Bass	$12.95

Favorite Movie Themes
13 themes, including: *An American Symphony* from Mr. Holland's Opus • Braveheart • Chariots of Fire • Forrest Gump – Main Title • Theme from *Jurassic Park* • Mission: Impossible Theme • and more.

00841166	Flute	$10.95
00841167	Clarinet	$10.95
00841168	Trumpet/Tenor Sax	$10.95
00841169	Alto Sax	$10.95
00841170	Trombone	$10.95
00841171	F Horn	$10.95
00841296	Violin	$10.95

Hymns for the Master
15 inspirational favorites, including: All Hail the Power of Jesus' Name • Amazing Grace • Crown Him with Many Crowns • Joyful, Joyful We Adore Thee • This Is My Father's World • When I Survey the Wondrous Cross • and more.

00841136	Flute	$12.95
00841137	Clarinet	$12.95
00841138	Alto Sax	$12.95
00841139	Trumpet	$12.95
00841140	Trombone	$12.95

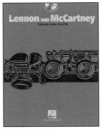

Lennon and McCartney Solos
Instrumentalists will love playing along with these 11 favorites: All My Loving • Can't Buy Me Love • Eleanor Rigby • The Long and Winding Road • Ticket to Ride • Yesterday • and more.

00841542	Flute	$10.95
00841543	Clarinet	$10.95
00841544	Alto Sax	$10.95
00841545	Tenor Sax	$10.95
00841546	Trumpet	$10.95
00841547	Horn	$10.95
00841548	Trombone	$10.95
00841549	Violin	$10.95
00841625	Viola	$10.95
00841626	Cello	$10.95

Motown Favorites
11 grooving hits from Motown, including: ABC • Heatwave • I Can't Help Myself • I Heard It Through the Grapevine • My Girl • Stop! In the Name of Love • You Can't Hurry Love • more.

00841768	Flute	$10.95
00841769	Clarinet	$10.95
00841770	Alto Sax	$10.95
00841771	Tenor Sax	$10.95
00841772	Trumpet	$10.95
00841773	F Horn	$10.95
00841774	Trombone	$10.95
00841775	Violin	$10.95
00841776	Viola	$10.95
00841777	Cello	$10.95

Movie & TV Themes
12 favorite themes, including: A Whole New World • Where Everybody Knows Your Name • Moon River • Theme from Schindler's List • Theme from Star Trek® • You Must Love Me • and more.

00841452	Flute	$10.95
00841453	Clarinet	$10.95
00841454	Alto Sax	$10.95
00841455	Tenor Sax	$10.95
00841456	Trumpet	$10.95
00841457	Trombone	$10.95
00841458	Violin	$10.95

Praise and Worship Solos
15 favorites: Blessed Be the Name • Come, Thou Fount of Every Blessing • Holy, Holy, Holy • I Stand Amazed in the Presence • Rejoice Ye Pure in Heart • To God Be the Glory • more.

00841373	Flute	$12.95
00841375	Alto Sax	$12.95
00841376	Clarinet	$12.95
00841377	Trumpet	$12.95
00841378	French Horn	$12.95
00841379	Trombone	$12.95

Sound of Music
9 songs with CD accompaniment so instrumentalists can play along with a real band. Songs include: Climb Ev'ry Mountain • Do-Re-Mi • Edelweiss • The Lonely Goatherd • Maria • My Favorite Things • Sixteen Going on Seventeen • So Long, Farewell • The Sound of Music.

00841582	Flute	$10.95
00841583	Clarinet	$10.95
00841584	Alto Sax	$10.95
00841585	Tenor Sax	$10.95
00841586	Trumpet	$10.95
00841587	Horn	$10.95
00841588	Trombone	$10.95
00841589	Violin	$10.95
00841590	Viola	$10.95
00841591	Cello	$10.95

1203